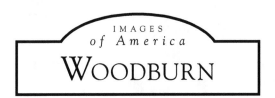

IMAGES
of America

WOODBURN

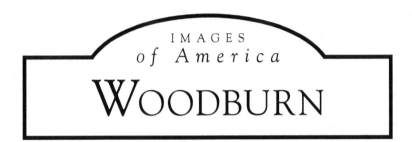

IMAGES
of America

WOODBURN

Beverlee Jory Koutny

ARCADIA
PUBLISHING

Published by Arcadia Publishing
Charleston, South Carolina

Library of Congress Control Number: 2011926552

For all general information, please contact Arcadia Publishing:
Telephone 843-853-2070
Fax 843-853-0044
E-mail sales@arcadiapublishing.com
For customer service and orders:
Toll-Free 1-888-313-2665

Visit us on the Internet at www.arcadiapublishing.com

This book is dedicated to Jesse Settlemier and all those early pioneers in Woodburn who helped create a prosperous and growing city in the heart of the Willamette Valley and miles from the mighty Willamette River.

CONTENTS

ACKNOWLEDGMENTS

This book was put together with the help of many people. However, the computer expertise of my daughters Nancy Eichsteadt and Cindy Allen was invaluable. Their technical skills and dedication to helping were essential for organizing the book. Donna Gramse, from the Woodburn Berry Museum, was a walking history resource. Thank you, Frank Sheers; Eddie Kahut; Richard Morris; Nancy and Loy Kirksey; Karen Ostrum; Ed Murphy; Russ Baglein; City of Woodburn; Dave Hegeman from the State Library Archives; Dan and Peggy Dinges, from Daniels Photography, who donated and scanned many of the pictures; Don and Rhonda Judson from the chamber of commerce; Salem Public Library; Dave Ellingson from Woodburn Academy of Art, Science and Technology; Norma Wilkerson; Lee Kellow; Margaret and Martin Krupika; Yes Graphics; Tom Sauvain; Brenda Diaz; Amalia Moreno; Ken Leonard; Woodburn Fire Department; Bill Coleman, for your expertise in Woodburn history; John Allen, who read the script for grammatical errors; and all those who received calls from me asking for information, help, and pictures. This book would not be possible without all of you. Your photographs and your stories have helped to piece together this short pictorial history of early Woodburn.

The following have furnished the photographs for this book: Oregon State Library (OSL); Woodburn Berry Museum (WBM); Daniel Dinges Photography (DDP); Richard Morris Photos of Russian Old Believers (RMP); Senior Estates photographer Ken Leonard (KLP); Salem Public Library (SPL); Cynthia Louise Allen (CLA), who provided technical support as well.

INTRODUCTION

In the beginning, the land in and around Woodburn was the home of the Kalapuya Indians. For hundreds of years, they roamed the area, moving to new locations for fresh fish, game, roots, and berries. One of their principle foods was the bulb of the camas plant, which grew on the prairie. This plant, a member of the lily family, was a universal staple of many different tribes on the prairie and was used for both barter and food. By 1822, the Indian population had been nearly wiped out by diseases brought by early white settlers. There were less than 500 Indians left in the Willamette Valley at the time of the first Oregon territorial census in 1850. And in 1855, the Indians remaining in the area were relocated to the Grand Ronde Indian Reservation.

Woodburn is situated on the eastern edge of an area known as the French Prairie, which had very few trees because of the Indian practice of burning the tall, tough, dry grass over hundreds of square miles in the autumn each year to make it sprout new shoots to feed their horses. This left deer and elk to find food in small unburned patches. In the process, small animals would jump out of the ring of fire and the Indians would trap them. The Indians carefully released a percentage of the animals back to the earth so there would be small animals for the next year. The fire and smoke were an aggravation, but it prevented the trees from growing in many places and made the prairie a good place to begin farming.

The first European settlers were French Canadian trappers who came in the 1820s and 1830s to retire on land given to them by Dr. John McLoughlin of the Hudson's Bay Company district headquarters at Fort Vancouver. Many of the trappers had Indian wives and were ready to retire and become farmers. They had brought their furs to trade at Fort Vancouver and met McLoughlin, who encouraged families to stay by giving them supplies, including wheat seed to help them get started. The French Catholic trappers welcomed the Catholic priests who arrived in the area in January 1839. Marriages were blessed, and the priests baptized many children.

The Oregon Country formed a provisional government after the early French Canadian fur trappers assembled with American pioneers to determine if the majority of settlers wanted to organize a government for the region. On May 2, 1843, at Champoeg, the first provisional government was established west of the Rocky Mountains. The vote was 52-50 for forming a government, with the American pioneers voting for representation from the United States and the French Canadians voting to become affiliated with England. Two French Canadians voted with the Americans.

In 1845, one of the early French Canadian settlers, Jean B. Ducharme, claimed the land that is now East Woodburn. Other pioneers in the area were Bradford Bonney, George Leisure, and Eli Cooley. Today, the town of Woodburn sits on land that was once owned by these men. Ducharme lost his large acreage, and it was bought at a sheriff's sale by Jesse Settlemier.

A new town was being cleared and developed just north of the settlement of Belle Passi and was first called Halsey, after a railroad officer. It was discovered that there was already a town by that name south of Albany, so the new town needed another designation. One story that has been verbally passed down is that E.P. Rogers, the assistant general passenger agent of the Southern Pacific Railroad, was watching a large pile of slashing being burned to clear land in the new town. He had the thought of naming the emerging city Woodburn, and the name stuck. Another theory is that a local resident ran around alerting people to an out-of-control burn by calling, "Wood burn, wood burn!" Stories abound, and here is one told by Charles E. Nebergall in 1981 that was passed down from his grandfather, a close friend of Jesse Settlemier in the 1880s.

> "Settlemier platted the town and left a large grove of fir trees surrounded by cleared fields. When the railroad came through, their right of way went directly through the middle of the grove. The felled trees and brush were left alongside the track until winter when they were burned. The fire got out of control, and a substantial quantity of the standing timber was destroyed along with the brush. The name Woodburn commemorated this happening."

A more practical version is that Jesse grew up in Alton, Illinois, near the small settlement of Woodburn, Illinois. Perhaps Jesse carried the name to Oregon. There are at least nine other towns named Woodburn in the United States.

The population of Woodburn has changed dramatically—from early European pioneers and French Canadian trappers to over 50-percent Hispanic, a community of Russians, and a large population of senior citizens today. The total population of Woodburn in the 2010 census is about 23,000. This does not count the area surrounding the city, where many farm families reside.

Spanish-speaking migrants came to work on the farms during World War II. Farmers began to find year-round work for them, and their families eventually joined them and began settling in. Russian immigrants came looking for a place to put down roots. They had been escaping persecution in Russia, China, Turkey, and other places for many years because of their religion. Seniors came looking for a golf course and affordable housing in a retirement community with individual homes. They founded Senior Estates Golf and Country Club, the ideal community. This population of active seniors has added immensely to the community by volunteering many talents to various worthwhile causes around Woodburn.

One

Belle Passi

Belle Passi was a small but thriving community on a well-used wagon road between Oregon City and Salem. Ten years before Woodburn was developed, this was the community where people came from near and far to shop and go to school.

Rev. Neill Johnson arrived over the Oregon Trail in 1848 and settled his family in this not-yet-named community, where he organized the Cumberland Presbyterian Church. Tradition says that Reverend Johnson liked a story he had read in his theology book about a place in Italy that he remembered as being called Belle Passi—"beautiful place" in Italian—and so the little settlement was given that name. Reverend Johnson was said to be a dynamic speaker, full of energy. The first church meetings were held in the log schoolhouse in the small settlement.

Church members eventually constructed a new two-story lumber building in 1857 that housed the church on the first floor and a new school on the second floor. Students came from miles around to board in the community and go to school in Belle Passi. There was a library full of good books. A post office was established in the community when a stagecoach line began carrying mail between Oregon City and Salem.

In 1852, a bizarre event occurred when a stranger wandered into the church during a sermon. He sat down on a bench and fell to the floor. The church members carried him across the street to the home of a Mr. Kennedy. There, they discovered that the man was dead. He had no identification. A Mr. Layman owned a plot of cleared land behind the school and offered it for burial of the stranger. The site became the Belle Passi Cemetery that is still in use today. A few years after the man was buried, some neighbors collected money and placed the name "William Eaton" on the stranger's tombstone. (No explanation is recorded for the origin of this name.)

The railroad chose to bypass Belle Passi, and people began moving to Woodburn and Gervais, causing the town to disappear into history. Only a school building and cemetery with the name of the former community remain.

Rev. Neill Johnson died at the age of 87 and is buried in Belle Passi Cemetery along with his wife, Esther Roelfson Johnson, and several of their children. This map shows the location of Belle Passi in relation to Woodburn. It is only about two miles south of downtown. On the right is Oregon Route 99E. (WBM.)

This is the Belle Passi Cemetery funeral of Jesse Settlemier in 1913. In the foreground is the footstone for Jesse's first wife, Eleanor. Jesse was a well-respected businessman and founder of the city of Woodburn. He retired to Portland with his third wife, Mary, while his eldest son, Frank, took over the operation of the nursery. Many people mourned Jesse's passing. (WBM.)

This monument in Belle Passi Cemetery is dedicated to the veterans of three different wars: the Civil War, the Spanish-American War, and the Indian Wars that were fought by early settlers against Native American tribes. The American Legion holds a service here each Memorial Day in honor of all veterans, and small flags decorate the graves of individual veterans while large flags line the access roads throughout the cemetery. (Courtesy of Cindy Allen.)

Here is one of the more unusual headstones in Belle Passi Cemetery. It marks the grave of a man who belonged to the Woodmen of the World fraternity. Someone fashioned a marker out of cement to resemble a log with an axe, a hammer, and a bird attached. It is a remarkable work of art. (SPL.)

Belle Passi Schoolhouse now stands as the only building remaining from the vanished town of Belle Passi. It housed a church in the basement and a school on the upper floor. A Russian group of Molokans holds church services here now and are one of the reasons the Russian Old Believers came to Woodburn. (WBM.)

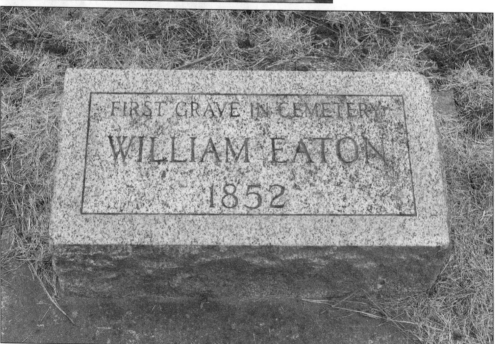

Here lies the first man to be buried in Belle Passi Cemetery. He had no identification on him when he died, so a few years later he was given the name of William Eaton, and a marker was placed on his grave. Belle Passi residents remembered him in death and gave him a properly marked resting place. (CLA.)

Two

BIRTH OF A DREAM

Jesse Settlemier was born February 5, 1840, in Alton, Illinois. The Settlemier family came west in 1849 over the Oregon Trail when Jesse was nine years old. They headed for the gold mines in California, where Jesse's mother and younger brother were victims of a flood near the Feather River. The site of their graves is unknown.

After he lost his wife and child, George Settlemier, along with his eight remaining children, including Jesse, decided to board the *Montague*, a ship headed for Oregon. After six weeks of waiting to cross the bar at Astoria and almost starving to death, the Settlemier family finally landed in Oregon and proceeded to Oregon City for the winter. There, George sprouted some tree seeds he had brought with him. He found a land grant in what is now the town of Mt. Angel and established the first plant nursery in Marion County.

Teenager Jesse and two brothers started a nursery in Talent, Oregon, and took turns walking back and forth to Mt. Angel on the weekends to bathe, get clean clothes, and bring back some home cooking.

At age 22, Jesse was anxious to begin his own nursery, so after marrying 16-year-old Eleanor C. Cochran on Christmas Day in 1862, and moving into a log cabin near where the present Settlemier House now stands, he bought 214 acres at $5 per acre at a sheriff's sale. In March 1863, he was well on his way to establishing his own business. Four of his children were born while Jesse and Eleanor lived in the log house.

A typical frame farmhouse was built next, which still stands on the corner of Arthur and Settlemier Streets. Three more children joined the family there. At the peak of his nursery success, Jesse discovered that the land he had purchased had a faulty title, and he was forced to buy the land again at a much higher assessed value after the case went to the US Supreme Court. Fortunately, Jesse had made some good business contacts, and the railroad company—most likely the Oregon and California Railroad—came to his rescue by loaning him the money he needed.

Jesse Settlemier gave away 50-foot-by-100-foot lots in his newly platted four-city-blocks to anyone who would improve upon the lot and move to his new city. He was growing a town and bringing people to work in his nursery. Settlemier donated land for a train depot and a school and constructed several buildings in town. Settlemier retired in 1892 and died in 1913. His eldest son, Frank, took over the nursery business. (DDP.)

The second Settlemier home was made of lumber. The seven Settlemier children grew up in this rather plain, but functional, farmhouse on the nursery property. It must have been a paradise for children to run around the farm. This house still stands and is in use across the street from the mansion. (DDP.)

Settlemier takes some time off to read a newspaper in front of his Queen Anne Victorian mansion, built in 1892 with a full basement and attic at a cost of $10,000. Perhaps he is reading the *Woodburn Independent*. Frank, the eldest son, did some remodeling of the house in 1912. He added a portico on the north side, cupboards in the dining room, and rearranged the indoor bathroom. (DDP.)

In 1871, his beloved Eleanor died, leaving Jesse with six daughters and one son—Ada, Nettie, Del, Emma, Elsie, Bess, and Frank. Jesse later married Clara S. Gray, who died six weeks later from typhoid fever. He then married Mary C. Woodworth from Howell Prairie, and they had one son, Jesse Holland Settlemier Jr. Pictured are, from left to right, (first row) Ada, Jesse Sr., Mary, and Frank; (second row) Nettie, Del, Emma, Jesse Jr., Elsie, and Bess. (WBM.)

Frank Settlemier inherited the mansion and lived there with his wife, Mable. They had no children. Frank was a strict taskmaster, and people who worked for him have said that he often watched out of an attic window in the big house to make sure the workers were doing their jobs. He and Mable were highly involved with the Masons and Eastern Star, respectively. (Left, DDP; right, OSL.)

Half-gas, half-electric lights were installed in the Settlemier House when it was first built. The lights in this picture are courtesy of Emmit Hemshorn, a historian who lives in the Settlemier neighborhood, and are still in working condition. Woodburn was the second city in Oregon to have electricity in 1892—after Portland and before Eugene. (CLA.)

These are a few of the many men who worked at the Settlemier Nursery. Many businesses were created by people to meet the demands of those who had moved to the town to work in the nursery. And Jesse was generous with his tree stock. He gave a tree to each family who would accept a lot in Woodburn and improve it. (WBM.)

Walnut Avenue, Woodburn, Oregon.

The location of Walnut Avenue was a mystery until someone discovered that there were walnut trees from the Settlemier Nursery planted along the street in front of the mansion. Walnut Avenue had been renamed Settlemier Avenue. Many original trees that were planted by Settlemier are still standing along Settlemier Avenue and in Settlemier Park. (WBM.)

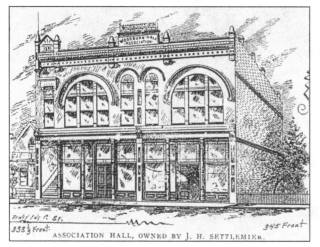

ASSOCIATION HALL, OWNED BY J. H. SETTLEMIER.

The Association Hall, built by Jesse Settlemier, was located on Front Street and divided into small business offices. In recent years, the building was home to the Salud Medical Center. The structure was severely damaged in the Spring Break earthquake of 1993 when the roof fell in. This building was also the site of a unique "turkey shoot" in the early years of the town. Live turkeys were thrown out of the second-story windows. People scrambled on the street to catch one for their Thanksgiving feast. (WBM.)

This is the Masonic Lodge, located on the corner of Arthur and Front Street in downtown Woodburn. It was built by Jesse Settlemier. He maintained his nursery stock in the winter by storing bare-rooted trees in the basement of the lodge in case there was a hard freeze. (OSL.)

Three

Development of
Transportation

Railroads were coming west, and one was going to miss the newly established city of Woodburn. Jesse purchased more land and gave 50 acres to the Oregon Electric Railroad, which built a track three miles west of Woodburn, and he gave 35 acres to the Oregon and California Railroad (later the Southern Pacific) that went through downtown Woodburn. Jesse laid out a town with four blocks next to the new railroad, and downtown Woodburn was established in 1871.

He gave the railroad one lot for a new depot. The depot building can be found today behind St. Luke's Catholic Church on Fourth Street. Many Chinese men were employed to build the railroad. They were not welcomed by white railroad workers and stayed out of the way when they were off duty, and there is still a den in a basement under First Street where they resided during their off-duty hours. A few started businesses.

The nursery business flourished because of easy access to transportation, and Woodburn Nursery was the largest in the Northwest. In 1892, there were three million plants sold, and the profit was around $60,000.

In 1919, Oregon adopted a gasoline tax to help with road-building, and by 1923, a north-south state highway was completed from Portland to the California border. It was the first border-to-border paved highway west of the Mississippi and was christened Pacific Highway 99E. Another name found on postcards of the era is "The road to a thousand wonders." An arch was placed across the highway proclaiming "Woodburn, World's Berry Center" in 1923. It was removed when the road was widened in 1933. Other businesses were spawned by the horseless carriage: garages, gas stations, taxis, car parts businesses, and, eventually, trucks for hauling and buses to carry people. Auto parks also appeared with a place to buy gas and groceries and to rent a tent for the night. Restrooms were also available.

The train station became the meeting place for the town and the heart of the city. People came to meet friends and family, to go shopping in the big city of Portland or Salem, and to just hang out where the action was. The train made it so much easier to get around and to get supplies in and out from long distances. (WBM.)

Downtown Woodburn had a variety ways to get around. People did a lot of walking, but they also had many choices, such as the new electric trolley as well as bicycles or a horse and buggy. (OSL.)

The inaugural ride on the new electric trolley was a much-celebrated event on January 1, 1910. Frank Settlemier was at the head of the ticket line to try out the new method of reaching West Woodburn. Train passengers going by on the main line had to stop and wave. This picture shows the trolley in trouble. It ran off the tracks and into the mud. (WBM.)

Two trains are standing on the tracks ready to make their daily runs. It took two engines to negotiate Hito ("high top") Hill near Aurora. There was a turnaround in Woodburn, and train crews would often spend the night at a Woodburn hotel. Woodburn became a real railroad hub—a place to repair engines and move railcars around. (Courtesy of Frank Sheers, from the Kleinschmitt Collection.)

Trains needed to take on water to make steam to run the engine. They could count on it being available in Woodburn. The windmill pumped the water into a holding tank so trains could fill up their boilers. The turnaround made it possible for trains to return easily to Portland. (WBM.)

Early steam engines pulled the passenger and freight cars on the railroad. This one is loaded with wood in back to feed the fire that boiled the water. This made the steam that drove the engine. Steam engines were a remarkable invention and spawned many different machines to make work easier for people. (WBM.)

The Woodburn Depot was a popular place in the center of town along Front Street. The building on the left was used for freight storage. Men pulled special handcarts around to move freight and suitcases. The trains also carried mail up and down the valley, and it was sorted in a special railroad car as the train moved along. (WBM.)

Train engines were hardworking machines. This is a southbound train going through Woodburn. Trains quickly became a popular way of traveling and an efficient way to move freight and people. This one is near Cleveland Street, where the trolley tracks can be seen approaching Front Street. Trains had a distinct whistle to warn of their approach to road crossings. (Courtesy of Frank Sheers, from the Kleinschmitt Collection.)

Woodburn was given this steam engine by Southern Pacific Railroad, and it is the project of a committee of railroad enthusiasts to maintain and restore it. The train signals in the background have been added to the site. The outdoor Woodburn Railroad Museum, next to the city water tower, is maintained by the City of Woodburn. (WBM.)

The newly-acquired steam engine was dedicated at a ceremony attended by local dignitaries on July 27, 1957. Leith Abbott from Southern Pacific Railroad and Lovett Smith from Portland Division gave speeches. A steam whistle came from Joe Serres's steam tractor to represent the steam engine's signal. State representative Winton Hunt was the master of ceremonies. (Courtesy of Frank Sheers, from the Kleinschmitt Collection.)

From 1923 to 1933, this arch, proclaiming Woodburn as the "World's Berry Center," greeted those traveling through town. Motorcycles also used the highway. A number of auto parks catering to motorists began to appear to accommodate those who found a need to stay overnight or rest while driving a distance. Travelers could rent a tent or sleep in their cars in addition to buying gas and food. (OSL.)

Nellie Muir (right) and Babe Golet have found a paved street to try out the latest fair-weather automobile. (OSL.)

Kung Kee Ran was one of the many Chinese men who came to Woodburn to work on the railroad. The Chinese workers were cheaper to hire and more efficient than any other group of people working in railroad construction. They were highly resented by white workers doing the same jobs. There was much rivalry between the two groups. (WBM.)

A few Chinese managed to set up businesses like laundries and tea shops. These businesses eventually disappeared because US immigration laws would not allow the Chinese people to get a legal green card and stay or send for family. A rickshaw sits in front of this laundry on Front Street. (WBM.)

This is one of the many businesses spawned by the new automobile industry. This gas station has a tow truck to bring cars in when they need to be repaired. It did not take long for men to know what to do when a car did not run, but getting in touch with the towing company or gas station was not easy if one were stranded on the road. (WBM.)

Farmers soon adapted automobiles to meet their farming needs. This truck is making a delivery to a local market. Country roads were rarely paved, and electricity took many years to reach farms, so a trip to town was carefully planned to sell produce and buy necessities. Sometimes, it meant getting a treat like ice cream or candy. (WBM.)

Horses and buggies could be rented, so why not cars? This photograph shows another example of new jobs created by the arrival of automobiles. Starting a car was a real science. It took a lot of cranking and coaxing. Getting to one's destination safely could be a bit risky depending upon the skill of the driver. (WBM.)

Woodburn Lumber Company found it practical to use a horse and buggy to deliver lumber around town. Instead of gas, it used real horsepower. This worked best on roads that were not yet paved. Many roads in and around town had six inches of dust in the summer and six inches of mud in the winter. (WBM.)

When cars came onto the scene, men became very creative in ways to utilize them. This owner is running a city delivery business with his vehicle that reads "City Delivery." A note in the margin of the original image says the delivery service was run by Ed Barnett. It was fast, efficient, and there was a real need for moving various items quickly about the city. The unidentified young lady is enjoying her trip around town. (WBM.)

Here is a picture of one of the early auto parks that began emerging with the advent of automobiles. There were usually a small market and gas station as well as tents to rent and outdoor restrooms. One could also park safely and rest for a few hours or for the night in the car. (WBM.)

Most people enjoy a parade, and Woodburn has had many of them, with Front Street being a main route. Kids have always been a big part of those parades. Dressing up, showing off pets, and advertising events were a part of growing up in the city. Come rain or shine, there was never a lack of an audience to view the entertainment. (WBM.)

Every year since 1983, the Iverson family has hosted a tulip festival on their farm east of Woodburn. It is a month-long event with a "wine down" at the end, where the tulip flowers are topped and people can play with the petals. There are always working steam tractors and modern gas-powered tractors in the field. (Courtesy of Rhonda Judson and Woodburn Chamber of Commerce.)

Four

GROWTH OF THE CITY

In 1888, the Oregon legislature passed the Layman Act, making it unlawful to sell liquors in less than one-gallon quantities without a license. To obtain a license, a majority of legal voters of a precinct had to agree upon the establishment of a saloon. The Layman Act was incorporated into the new charter of the City of Woodburn, and a local saloon had to close its doors.

Emotions ran high, and many predicted the city would disappear without a saloon in town. Some went so far as to threaten a boycott of businesses. One business owner reduced his inventory and offered to sell his property because he was certain the town would vanish. Never before had a village on French Prairie been denied a saloon. Saloons drew customers and other stores benefited from people coming. For a few months, it seemed that the pessimists were right, but gradually cooler tempers prevailed.

Most lot titles in the new town were written to revert back if a saloon were established on the property. The prayer on the lips of many citizens was "Lead us not into temptation." The stated object of the law was to remove temptation and evil influences from the young and from the older citizens who might neglect their work, their families, and their businesses.

The town of Woodburn was finally incorporated in 1889. It was slow to get started, but when the Oregon and California Railroad Company completed its railway, things began to pick up. The city gave the railroad a subsidy.

When the first downtown buildings were constructed, there was very little space between them. Every block in town, except for one, was eventually destroyed by fire. That one block—between Cleveland and Arthur Streets—contained a livery stable full of dry straw and oil lamps. It never burned. Fires struck in 1893, 1896, and 1909, all before a fire department was officially organized in 1915. During the conflagrations, all that could be done was to rescue merchandise and try to keep the blaze from spreading with bucket brigades.

Seen in this 1893 image, Front Street in downtown Woodburn was the place to be. The road is not paved, but the trains were running at this time. The West Side School (on the far right), with a bell tower on top, is located on First Street. The building with the small bell tower in the center left on Front Street is the first schoolhouse, which was moved to that location to make way for the new grade school on First Street. (OSL.)

Here is a bird's-eye view of Front Street from the water tower. The West Side School building, at far right, was a state-of-the-art facility for its time. It was later torn down and replaced by Lincoln School, which gave way to the current post office building in July 1972. (WBM.)

M&F Grocery replaced Safeway in downtown Woodburn when Safeway closed its doors in 1942. Most businesses had small storefronts and long, narrow rooms inside. It was the era before superstores, and one would shop at the bakery, at the meat market, and at the fruit and vegetable shop. Later, grocery stores expanded to include all departments under one roof. (WBM.)

This view of Front Street shows the Association Building in the middle. The street is still not paved, but the train is running, and people are waiting for it to arrive. In the foreground is one of the handcarts used to haul baggage and freight. The town probably found it hard to contain the excitement of such a modern transportation service. (WBM.)

Cleveland Street is located on the south edge of Woodburn's city center. It was a very active street with train tracks running out to West Woodburn. The armory building is in the left background. Boxcars are stored on one lot, and the new bank building is on the corner of Front Street and Arthur Street. A Chinese laundry has a rickshaw parked in front. (WBM.)

Early Front Street was a natural gathering place for townspeople. Here, it is unpaved but well traveled. The people are dressed in their Sunday best to go shopping downtown. One never knew whom he might meet. The Woodburn Hotel is clearly visible on First Street. By 1975, the street would be paved, the buildings made of brick, and cars would be moving about. (DDP.)

There were several hotels in town where travelers could stay while doing business or visiting the city. The Woodburn Hotel was also used by the train crews that stayed overnight. The site became a parking lot in back of Handy's Market when the hotel was torn down. It was the first parking lot connected to a business in town. (WBM.)

Smallman Hotel was another of the lodgings where travelers could rest. It was located on Cleveland Street between Second Street and Settlemier Avenue and owned by two women. Crews often stayed overnight at the hotels in Woodburn before resuming their duties on the trains. (WBM.)

The armory building was between First and Second and Cleveland and Montgomery Streets. It covered a complete block. Every year, firemen sponsored a dance on Thanksgiving night in the armory when people came home to Woodburn for the holidays. It was a fundraiser for their organization. (OSL.)

After the old armory building was dismantled, a new armory was put up on Park Avenue. Many community events are still held in this structure, and for a number of years it was home to the Marion County Fair. Many Marion County residents brought their prize animals and freshly-preserved fruits and vegetables to compete for ribbons. (DDP.)

The fair was always well attended. Everyone enjoyed visiting neighbors and looking at the prize fruits, vegetables, animals, and baked goods. People enjoyed showing off the best of the summer harvest, and competition was keen for ribbons and trophies. The yearly fair has since moved to the Oregon State Fairgrounds in Salem. (WBM.)

Andrew Carnegie was a Scotsman who acquired immense wealth through hard work. His foundation built many libraries around the world and gave money to Woodburn for the library building located on Garfield Street. Later additions have been made while still preserving the original structure. (DDP.)

The Bungalow Theatre opened its doors in 1910 on Front Street. Irv Westenscow closed the Bungalow and opened the Pix Theatre on First Street between Grant and Hayes Streets in 1947. The Bungalow Theatre remains as part of the Woodburn Berry Museum on Front Street today. (WBM.)

The Pix Theater showed the very latest movies, and there was always a double feature that one could attend, complete with cartoons and a newsreel. The marquee advertises a double show of *The Grapes of Wrath* and *Tobacco Road*. Eventually, the Pix Theatre began showing only Spanish-language films. It finally closed and was sold to a furniture company. (WBM.)

Handy's Market was everyone's favorite downtown grocer—friendly and helpful clerks, good prices, and a nice location with a parking lot in the heart of downtown Woodburn citizens made this business a popular shopping stop. It was the first business to maintain a parking lot in back of the store. (DDP.)

Inside, grocery stores looked very different from present-day supermarkets, and many of them specialized in one type of food only, like a bakery or meat market. Handy's Market had it all under one roof, including a frozen-food section. One-stop shopping would save the homemaker a lot of time. (WBM.)

Horde Grocery in downtown Woodburn was typical of grocery stores of the 1910 era. One would take a grocery list and give it to the clerk, who would scurry around and find the items. The floors were oiled wood with no carpets or rugs on them. Some stores were cash-and-carry; others would allow customers to charge and pay by the month. (WBM.)

Safeway had a presence in downtown Woodburn for a short time, and it would have looked like this store in Salem. A meat market is in the back. The parent company of Safeway had many mergers and eventually left downtown Woodburn to show up later in Fairway Plaza on the edge of Senior Estates in the 1960s before moving to Mount Hood Avenue and Highway 99E at two different locations. (WBM.)

Grover's Drug Store was a classy joint with a linoleum floor. The floor was not typical for the times. Most drugstores in the early 1900s had a soda fountain and a place to sit and sip a soda or have some ice cream. There was a big demand for tobacco items, pictured in the foreground. (WBM.)

Founded in 1898, Sowa's Foundry on Young Street in downtown Woodburn was always a busy place. There were always farm machinery and various items to fix. Bending steel and other metals was hard work. Paul Sowa died in a machine accident while working one day in 1938, one month before his son, Paul Jr., was born. (DDP.)

The First National Bank had a presence in downtown Woodburn for many years until it closed its doors for good. It was first located on Front Street in the Association Building and later moved into new quarters at Garfield and First Streets. Still later, it changed hands and became part of Wells Fargo Bank. (WBM.)

The Bromhoff Bakery owners built the Coe Building in 1911. But, as with many businesses in that era, the bakery moved many times and occupied many different store spaces in town. The Coe Building was rented to a church and later became a part of a manufacturer that still makes metal stirrups for saddles. (WBM.)

A salesman tried to talk a businessman into becoming a franchise dealer of a horseless carriage. The businessman was skeptical and said no. There were no roads for such a product to use. The salesman did not make a sale. He was offering a Model T Ford franchise. Sauvain Ford Motor Company took on the challenge and sold Ford cars on the corner of Front and Harrison Streets for many years. (DDP.)

In 1892, a new business came to town next to the railroad tracks, the three-story Woodburn Feed Mill. A steam engine moved the machinery and made electricity for lights in the mill and also for streetlights on Front Street. One hundred barrels of flour were produced every a day and labeled White Rose and Snow Drop. Today the business has changed from a feed-and-seed operation to a fertilizer products manufacturing plant. (WBM.)

Norman's Service Center was the place to buy Ford tractors, and every farmer wanted one. This was a good business to have in the era when farmers were looking for ways to get more work done in less time. Tractors revolutionized agriculture. (DDP.)

In 1907, a city ordinance was passed that all stores had to be built of brick to prevent serious fires like those that had destroyed whole blocks in the core area of town in the past. This is the Walter Tooze Block. Tooze was involved in several businesses in downtown Woodburn and became known as "The Produce and Merchant King of French Prairie." (WBM.)

F. Miller Insurance was in this building, which burned. It was where the First National Bank later located on First and Garfield Streets. Structures made of wood were not practical, as whole blocks would burn once a fire got started. Bucket brigades tried to keep nearby buildings from catching fire, and people also helped remove merchandise in nearby stores. (WBM.)

Valley Manufacturing Company is the oldest business still operating in downtown Woodburn. The company occupies part of the Coe Building on First and Arthur Streets. It manufactures horse stirrups and pack saddles that are sent all over the country. Flomer's Furniture uses a portion of this building for storing furniture today. (WBM.)

O.D. "Scotty" Henderson (right) operated a harness shop in Woodburn. He was a commander in the National Guard and led Woodburn troops into the Philippines during the Spanish-American War. He acted as a marshal when called upon and was killed when a fugitive fired upon him during a night chase. He was both well known and well liked, so his funeral attracted a large crowd. (WBM.)

Perds' Pool Hall was one of the early businesses in downtown Woodburn. These businesses were commonly called "confectionaries." People could play pool and cards as well as drink liquor. Obviously, the laws against taverns had taken a new turn since the early days, as they were allowed downtown. (WBM.)

This was the first US post office in Woodburn, located on Grant Street downtown. It is a block east of the present post office and was a great addition to the area. The mail had been handled in various buildings in the downtown area before it had a home of its own. (WBM.)

The new post office, located on Grant Street between First and Second Streets, was designed well. It was built south of the old Lincoln Elementary School. The interior was elegant. There was no street delivery, so everyone who wanted mail delivered had to rent a box in the post office. (WBM.)

This is a view of Front Street looking west on Young Street. Several buildings had to be removed to make room for a continuation of the street across the tracks, but the new roadway was named Garfield Street, as it did not quite line up with Young Street. The Masonic Lodge and the Woodburn Bank Building can be seen on the left. (WBM.)

Front Street in Woodburn was a bustling place in the 1920s. Brick buildings replaced wooden ones, and more cars were owned by residents. The trolley was still running, but its operation was coming to an end as cars became more affordable. The buildings with decorative pediments bear the names of the builders. The Association Building housed the First National Bank. (WBM.)

This mill was located on Cleveland Street on the edge of the town, and it cut many board feet of lumber for building houses and businesses in and around Woodburn. These were the days when old-growth trees could be logged in nearby hills and brought into the mill for processing. (WBM.)

A volunteer fire department was organized in September 1901, but it had little equipment to fight a large fire. A bond measure was passed in 1911, and Woodburn purchased a water plant with a 6,000-gallon storage tank. In 1915, a city-sanctioned volunteer fire department was finally established. The firemen in this picture are, from left to right, Ray Hicks, Sidney Tomlinson, Bill Pennybaker, Fred Dase, Raymond Mosberger, and Henry Bomhoff. (OSL.)

Margaret and Martin Krupika are riding in a 1923 fire engine. Floyd "Speed" Maricle was Woodburn's first paid fire chief from 1953 to 1960. Martin was then hired and served the city well for 26 years from 1960 to 1986. In 1976, the fire district headquarters station was dedicated to Joe P. Sowa, elected volunteer chief from 1943 to 1953. (Courtesy of Martin Krupika.)

Woodburn City Hall was located on First Street and Lincoln Street. The fire department had quarters on the right side at street level. The police department was on the left side in the basement. Other city offices were located in the upstairs offices. The building is now empty and up for sale. A new city hall is located at Second and Arthur Streets. (WBM.)

Bargains galore for everyone in the family could be purchased at this attractive store on Front Street. Notice the new sweaters on the front table. There were not many choices for buying clothing in downtown Woodburn. But an excursion on the train took one to the cities of Portland or Salem, where many of the latest styles were available. (WBM.)

How many men does it take to fix an electric line? Guess we'll never know. Perhaps these men simply wanted some attention and their picture taken. The question is how did they get down without a ladder? The light poles in this era had glass insulators to hold the wires. (WBM.)

Austin's Grocery was located at Front and Grant Streets in downtown Woodburn. People generally cooked from scratch and just bought necessities like flour, sugar, and sometimes oat cereal. Many fruits and vegetables were home-canned from the garden for winter use. Meat was homegrown, or one could go to the butcher shop. Bread was usually made fresh at home. (DDP.)

In the early morning, fresh bread smells were emitted all over town from the Home Bakery. The business relocated several times into different buildings around town. Housewives enjoyed the availability of fresh bread and saved some time in the kitchen. (WBM.)

J.R. Landon and Son Furniture and Jewelry was one of those stores that offered more than one business in the same space. The post office was also located in this building before it moved to its own structure. (WBM.)

National Guardsmen are assembled to take the train to Salem and then to San Francisco, where they set sail for the Philippines during the Spanish-American War. Capt. John Poorman was in charge. The boys from Woodburn made a big contribution to the winning of the war. (WBM.)

The Becker family was very innovative and hardworking. One Becker brother had a garage in downtown Woodburn on First Street, while another had a pool hall in front of the garage on Front Street. A third brother grew tobacco, dried it, and made Oregon and Willamette cigars to sell in the East. (WBM.)

Many stately homes once graced the streets of Woodburn at the turn of the century, and many have since disappeared. In this 1912 picture, this house, owned by Albert and Mary Loveridge, is on Second Street across from the library and was built in 1893. Cheryl and Frank Lonergan currently call it home. (Courtesy of Cheryl and Frank Lonergan.)

Five

INNOVATIVE EDUCATION

Woodburn had a school before it had a city hall. One school was located on North Boones Ferry Road. It was called Hall Grade School. In 1885, a one-room frame building was constructed on First Street between Lincoln and Grant Streets with a belfry and bell on top. Jesse Settlemier donated the land. To accommodate more children a few years later, two rooms were added, one on each side.

In 1891, it was decided to build a new school on First Street, and West Side School was constructed. It was a state-of-the-art edifice with a built-in heating system. Students lined up outside and marched to drum beats as they entered the school. Three rooms were on the left and three on the right. The first floor held six grades. Upstairs were the seventh and eighth grades plus the library and auditorium. There were eight rooms with an average of 50 students in each. Two school boards met one evening a month. One was in charge of school business; the second discussed discipline. There was no local high school at this time. A two-year course beyond the eighth grade was offered in 1901, but most high school students went off to a larger city for further education. In 1905, an 11th grade was added, with plans to add a 12th grade if there was a need. The high school was on the second floor.

In 1908, a one-room school on Lincoln Street became the first high school. It had 83 students and a faculty of two teachers, Maude E. McKinley and Albert Frost. The East Side School was located on Gatch Street where the Bible Baptist Church was eventually built.

Woodburn High School needed more room, so in 1916 it moved to a two-story building that is now the site of Washington Grade School on Lincoln Street. Meanwhile, in 1930, the West Side School at First and Grant Streets was torn down and the one-story Lincoln Grade School built on the site. Grades seven and eight moved to the new high school on Lincoln Street.

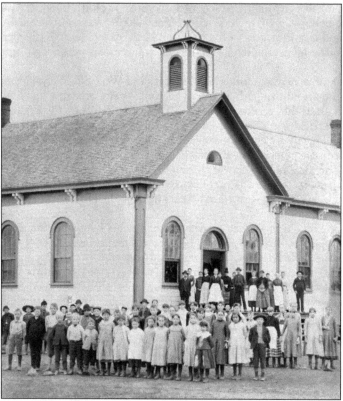

There were small country schools located all around the outskirts of Woodburn in early times. They often had one room and one teacher. Children had to walk to reach them in all kinds of weather. A typical lunch might be homemade bread and jam. (WBM.)

The first downtown school was located on First Street between Lincoln and Grant Streets. It originally had one room, but this soon proved too small. Two rooms were added, one on the right and one on the left side of the original building. Later, the structure was moved and a new school took its place. (WBM.)

The three-room school was replaced by West Side School from 1909 to 1925; it was a state-of-the-art, two-story facility with a built-in heating system and a school bell on top. In 1930, the school district reached out with free bus transportation to students from Butteville, Aurora, Monitor, and Whiskey Hill. (WBM.)

The West Side School class of 1920 is assembled in front of the school. The building was torn down in 1925 to make room for Lincoln Grade School, which was a one-story building that stretched out to accommodate many classrooms. (WBM.)

Auditorium - Woodburn High School

The second floor of the West Side School contained an auditorium. This is what it looked like when packed with schoolchildren in 1914. The average classroom had 50 students. (WBM.)

Bus service began with a bus fee for those coming from farm areas over gravel roads and dusty lanes to get to schools. District boundaries were much larger than they are today, reaching out to Champoeg Creek to the west and Butte Creek to the east. Kids hang out the bus windows in this picture of the one-story Lincoln School on First Street. (OSL.)

Lincoln School teachers were young and talented. Principal Nellie Muir, who later had a grade school named for her, is third from right. It must have been fun for children and teachers to work in a spacious new school. (WBM.)

Woodburn High School finally had a big, two-story, modern building of its own on Lincoln Street. The home economics class prepared lunch for about 20 students. The rest of the 200 students brought sack lunches from home with sandwiches made from either mom's homemade bread or slices from the 20¢ loaf from the store. (WBM.)

The high school band is assembled on the steps of the school. Many students learned to play musical instruments and continued playing in community bands after leaving school. Bands were called upon to march in parades and entertain in the many community celebrations throughout the year. (WBM.)

The new stadium in Legion Park was where many high school athletic games took place. High school sports fans enjoyed the small roof during bad weather. The crowd of fans always helped to keep the local team going. And there were some very outstanding athletes who played on Woodburn teams. (DDP.)

French Prairie Middle School is located on the corner of Highway 214 and Boones Ferry Road in the former Woodburn High School building (the second location of the high school). Lincoln Grade School moved from First Street downtown to the same campus to share facilities. Both schools are still located there today. (DDP.)

Washington School grew out of the first Woodburn High School building on Lincoln Street. The second story of the high school sustained damage from a fire and was removed, making the new grade school a one-story building. It is in operation today. (DDP.)

A new grade school, Nellie Muir School, was built on Hayes Street in Woodburn. Muir never lived to see the educational facility that bears her name. Today, this school sends notes about school activities home to parents in three languages—English, Spanish, and Russian. (DDP.)

St. Benedict Parochial School opened October 5, 1903, with grades one through eight. It was a two-story building with a basement, and the Benedictine Sisters from Mt. Angel staffed the school, which was torn down in 1960 when the new St. Luke Grade School (pictured) took its place to the west of the church. A kindergarten has been added in later years. (DDP.)

Woodburn High School teacher Dave Ellingson shows off a 13,000-year-old bison bone, the biggest one ever discovered in the world. It was uncovered in 2006 near a small creek that meanders through the campus. Students are working on putting the huge skeleton back together with the help of professionals. (Courtesy of Dave Ellingson.)

Woodburn High School students actually get to sift through dirt and uncover real bones from a genuine archaeological site. Many interesting remains of extinct animals, including a giant sloth and a teratorn (bird), have been uncovered along Mill Creek. Here, David Robles is displaying his finds. (Courtesy of Dave Ellingson.)

Woodburn High School recently divided itself into four separate and distinct schools with four principals to better meet the needs of today's students. A number of students are also striving for a diploma in an international baccalaureate program. (CLA.)

The MacLaren Youth Correctional Facility has been in Woodburn since 1926. Project POOCH is a special program there that helps to teach responsibility, love, patience, and accomplishment to the young men fortunate enough to be assigned to the program. The boys are responsible for training stray dogs to become adoptable pets. (Courtesy of Joan Dalton.)

Six

RELIGIOUS FOUNDATIONS

Around 1872, the Cumberland Presbyterian Church building was moved from Belle Passi to the new city of Woodburn, about two miles north. The roads were very rough, so it was decided to use the railroad tracks to slide the building along. A train, belching smoke, arrived behind the building at noon and was unhappily held up while the moving foreman gave the workers a lunch break. The structure eventually arrived at its new home on First and Grant Streets in the newly established town of Woodburn.

For many years, Cumberland Presbyterian Church generously shared its meeting rooms with other congregations, including the "Other Presbyterian," the Methodist Episcopal, the Episcopalian, and the Seventh Day Adventist churches until those congregations were established in buildings of their own. In 1904, the Woodburn Presbyterian Church and the Cumberland Presbyterian Church merged and built a new church at Third and Garfield Streets. The new name of the combined congregations was the First Presbyterian Church of the U.S.A., now First Presbyterian Church.

The old Cumberland Presbyterian Church building was sold to the postal service and was then moved to face Front Street where it was used as a post office. An opera house was built on the lot where the church had stood and was used by schools as well as townspeople for an assembly building. After the merger, the Woodburn Presbyterian Church building was used as the city hall and firehouse, with a bell installed to call firefighters. A new bell was purchased which was louder, and it was placed on a high tower. A modern electric siren later replaced the bell. After many years of service, the old Cumberland Presbyterian Church building was torn down, and the lumber was made into a barn on the Eckhout farm near Woodburn.

A few of the earlier churches in Woodburn are mentioned in this chapter. The many Hispanic congregations and Russian prayer halls are new additions to the religious scene.

The Woodburn Christian Church was first located at East Lincoln and Doud Streets. It organized in 1901. In 1906, Brother Stevens arrived from Portland. Through his efforts and labor, a church building was completed. In 1919, a new church was completed. Property was purchased in Smith Addition on Workman Drive, and a third church structure was dedicated on December 11, 1966. The church building now houses the Iglesia Pentecostes congregation. (WBM.)

The Episcopal church was located very early (before the turn of the 20th century) on Lincoln Street. It was later a Christian Science Reading Room and is currently used by a Hispanic congregation, La Luz del Mundo. It was across the street from the First Christian Church. (WBM.)

The Church of God membership is assembled on the steps of its old church building. A new church was later located on Third Street. It has moved to Hoodview Street today and has become one of the very active congregations in town. A campground for this church was for many early years on Hardcastle Street near the railroad tracks. (WBM.)

The Church of God building on Third Street was purchased by the City of Woodburn when the congregation moved to Hoodview Avenue. The city used it for offices and a community center. It was later condemned because of plumbing and electrical issues and sold to a private owner. (DDP.)

Every year in the summer, the Church of God held camp meetings where 100 people or more camped out and attended gatherings dealing with Church doctrine. There were organized recreation, fun, and games for the whole family. The camp meetings eventually moved to Brooks. (WBM.)

Mid-Valley Community Church was first built around the East Side School that was on this site. An alternative school, Arthur Academy, now uses the church facilities during the week. (DDP.)

The First Methodist Episcopal Church was located on Young Street across from Wolfer's Heating. It burned and was replaced. The congregation eventually built a new church on Cascade Drive and renamed it the United Methodist Church. (WBM.)

The new United Methodist Church was built on the site of the original Methodist sanctuary. A building later erected on Cascade Drive offered plenty of room inside and parking around the outside. The new church building is used for many community events including an exceptional program of monthly musical concerts in the winter. (WBM.)

The Immanuel Lutheran congregation began August 15, 1909, when the first service on record was held in the home of L.E. Peterson on Young Street. The first church building was constructed at Oswald and Doud Streets. In 1954, ground was broken for a new church and parsonage on Lincoln Street, dedicated in August 1959. The Dorcus Ladies Aid organization carried much of the financial obligation. (WBM.)

The Presbyterian church was a wooden church building in 1930 in downtown Woodburn. The congregation purchased land on the corner of Boones Ferry Road and Highway 214 and built a new church in 1962. Following their mission statement, members have provided "a warm, welcoming, Christian fellowship" to the Woodburn Head Start, the Meals on Wheels program, the North Marion Senior Center, and a Spanish-speaking ministry. (WBM.)

The Most Reverend Archbishop F. N. Blanchet started a Catholic mission church in Woodburn. As with many different congregations, services were first held in private homes or rented halls. Property was eventually acquired, and a church building made of lumber was started in October 1899. The church was dedicated on October 20, 1901. Hop fields lie in the distance. (WBM.)

The wooden church was torn down and a brick church building constructed and named in honor of St. Luke in 1930. The bell tower was damaged in the 1993 Spring Break earthquake and had to be taken down, brick by brick, and rebuilt. Today, there are masses celebrated in both English and Spanish at the church. (DDP.)

71

St. Mary's Episcopal Church is located on West Hayes Street next to Nellie Muir School. The first service held in this new church was January 9, 1966. The old Episcopal church was at 195 East Lincoln Street, where the Christian Science church occupied the building for a while after the Episcopalians moved. The older church is now used by Iglesia Del Dios Vivo. (WBM.)

The Church of Jesus Christ of Latter-day Saints was first built on Bryan Street. The church and property were sold to a Hispanic congregation, Templo Gethsemani – Apostolic Church of Jesus Christ. Then, a new building was constructed by the Mormons on Country Club Road. The Mormons have a research library for genealogists and are currently helping to take care of a large community-sponsored garden. (DDP.)

The Woodburn Foursquare Church began in 1928 with a small group of believers who met in the Coe Building in downtown Woodburn. In 1931, it was granted a charter. The first church building was erected in 1935 and located on Park and Hardcastle Streets. The current building dates from 1953. There have been several remodels and changes over the years. (Both, courtesy of the Woodburn Foursquare Church.)

Old Building 1931 - 1953

Faith Christian Fellowship began as the Independent Full Gospel Church in 1935. Services were held in the Coe Building on Second and Montgomery Streets. In 1945, the church became affiliated with the Assembly of God. In 1964, a new building was constructed on Young Street, and in 1992 Woodburn School District began renting the school annex for Woodburn Success, an alternative–high school program. (Courtesy of Faith Christian Fellowship.)

The Nazarene Church was founded in 1969. The congregation purchased a large acreage in West Woodburn to hold camp meetings. Some land was sold off in the eastern part for a mobile home park. The church building was completed in 1972. Each Thanksgiving, volunteers put together a very large meal for all those who want to celebrate the holiday together. (WBM.)

The Woodburn Spanish Seventh-Day Adventist Church is located in West Woodburn. The Nazarene church owned the area at one time and sold lots for modular homes. Eventually, most of the land owned by the Nazarene church was developed into single-family homes. (WBM.)

Seven

LOCAL FARMING

The climate was perfect for many crops that did not require irrigation, such as grains, hops, corn, hay, loganberries, blackcaps, raspberries, evergreen blackberries, and flax. A few farmers even tried growing different crops such as tobacco and dandelion seed. Most years, it rained enough to keep the farm produce growing. Everyone tended large gardens and canned produce for winter use. A variety of animals were also raised on the farm—cattle, hogs, sheep, and chickens. A farmer's wife often sold chicken eggs to earn spending money.

In 1881, three French Prairie farmers discovered that they could make money with hops, which were used to flavor beer. Hops became the first local farm crop harvested by men, women, and children. Around Labor Day, whole families would schedule their vacations and board a train for Woodburn, where farmers would meet them with a wagon or buggy and take them to the farm to camp out and pick hops for a week or two.

Hops were first trained on poles to grow up and onto strings that were stretched between the poles. The pickers would harvest all the hops they could reach and then call for the "pole puller" so they could pick the hops on the higher strings. The hop poles were actually pulled out of the ground and laid down. When a basket was full, another worker was called to empty it into a box or sack. Yet another employee was summoned to weigh the sack of hops.

During Prohibition, many hops were plowed under. The only people using hops were those making home brew. The hop industry revived when beer was again a legal beverage, and Oregon hops led the world in quality and flavor.

Today, the calls of "wireman (to lower the vines)," "pole puller (to remove the poles)," and "basket full (to call the basket emptier)" are gone. Hop baskets are found only in antique stores, and the "weigher man" is no longer needed. Now, machines gather the hops from the field and bring them to a stationary picker. A way of life has vanished.

Barn raisings were not just in storybooks. Neighbors got together and constructed the barn for a family. Some of these are still standing, while others have disappeared due to neglect over the years. Most barns are no longer used for grain storage. Some shelter farm animals, but it is expensive to keep up a large barn when smaller farm buildings work just as well. (WBM.)

Making hay was a tedious task, and weather was always a factor in the success of the venture. Rain could cause the hay to mold in the field after it was cut. It had to dry before being stored for winter use. The farmer had to be good at predicting weather changes. (WBM.)

Farm homes were quite self sufficient. Hand pumps delivered cool, clear water ,which was heated on a big woodstove. The heated water was used for everything from cooking to washing clothes to bathing. Some homes had inside hand pumps in a sink, and there were stoves with water tanks built in, so when the stove was in use, the water would get hot. (OSL.)

If a farmer needed more horsepower, he simply hitched another horse or two to the item he wanted to move. Horses were valuable additions on every farm until steam engines and tractors began doing some of the work and replacing them. With proper care, a good work horse would live for 20 years. (WBM.)

Edward Becker experimented with growing tobacco plants. He processed the dried leaves and made tobacco that was fashioned into cigars and marketed in the eastern United States under the labels Oregon Cigars and Willamette Cigars. Some of his dried tobacco leaves can be found at the Woodburn Berry Museum. (WBM.)

There were several livery stables around town where farmers could rent animals and/or wagons to aid in farm work and hauling goods to market. This one is Bunning Dray Line. Livery stables disappeared along with draft horses after cars became more available. (WBM.)

Pole beans were picked by hand over several weeks. If they were to be sold to a cannery, the cannery usually told the farmer when to plant, so the crop could be harvested and processed while the beans were fresh. Today, bush beans are planted and harvested all at one time by machine. (WBM.)

Whole families would come out from the city to pick berries when they were ripe in the summer or fall. They would either stay in tents or in hastily made cabins on the farm. This was an opportunity to breathe fresh air, make a few dollars, and enjoy something different in vacations for a week or two. (DDP.)

This is crew of pickers posing in a field of loganberries. The field would be harvested several times over in the few weeks that the berries were ripening. Whole families spent the day in the field, and many took advantage of the fresh berries by sampling them as they picked. (DDP.)

Not everyone lived in houses, especially during a berry- or hop-picking vacation from the city. This tent was probably very comfortable in the fresh air of the country. All this picture lacks is a campfire. Living in the country for a few weeks in the summer was a healthy and reasonably inexpensive getaway. (WBM.)

Flower bulbs were raised throughout the valley and are still grown today. This is a field of daffodils along Highway 99E. The Iverson family started growing tulip bulbs on their farm east of Woodburn, and there is now a big tulip festival every year in March and April when the flowers are in bloom. (WBM.)

Whole families gathered in the hop fields to pick the ripe hops. It was quite a tedious job, separating the small green hops from the scratchy vines. Children picked some and played a lot with the other children in the days before child labor laws prevented them from being in the fields. (WBM.)

There are not many children in this hop-picking crew. They were probably not invited to be in the picture. Women did not usually wear slacks or jeans in turn-of-the-century times. The hop juice would stain clothing, and the scratchy vines would cause wounds. Some wore gloves and others would wind tape on their fingers. (WBM.)

Hops were poured from wooden baskets into burlap sacks and weighed. Occasionally a "dirty picker" would be caught with vines and dirt clods in the basket, which made it weigh more. Workers had to take time out to clean their hops as buyers would not buy them with too many vines and leaves. (WBM.)

There was a real art to drying the hops properly. This crew looks like it knows what it is doing at the hop dryer— besides posing for pictures. Sulfur was used to help take the moisture out of the hops, and the smell was sometimes overwhelming. It is no longer used in the drying process. (WBM.)

Whole families worked at picking hops in season. The unidentified woman on the left is properly dressed to keep from getting scratched by the hop vines. She has gloves to protect her hands and long sleeves to guard her arms. It was rare in the early days for women to wear pants. Perhaps these overalls were borrowed from a male member of the family. (OSL.)

Hop driers were invented by hop farmers to cure their crop before the hops were baled and stored for use in flavoring beer. Heat was supplied by a stove in the bottom of the building, and the hops were spread on a floor in the top of the drier for about 18 hours. Moisture escaped through vents in the roof. (OSL.)

Canneries began appearing in the early 1940s. Ray Brown Cannery later became Ray Mailing. Canneries loaned seeds to the farmers and told them when to plant so they would have a staggered crop of corn, beans, cabbage, brussels sprouts, pumpkins, peas, and other row crops to process. This is a bird's-eye view of Ray Mailing Cannery before Birds Eye Cannery came to town. (WBM.)

ery crew was mostly women
e jobs were seasonal. There
men who were managers and
d the machinery. Canning
sometimes messy labor, so
f aprons kept the workers dry.
men still did not wear slacks or
y kind while working. They were
d to wear hair nets. (WBM.)

me on the scene.
their crops. There
Bir
were i.
y, while women worked on belts
to remove stems, leaves, and into the cans. (DDP.)

North Marion Fruit

West Coast Fruit Growers Corporation, North Marion Fruit Company, and Smuckers also developed businesses locally. North Marion Fruit Company dealt mainly with berries and berry farmers. It also created part-time jobs to help the local economy. Berries were very fragile and needed to be handled quickly, usually during the night after they were picked during the day. In the beginning, berries were canned. Later, freezing berries became popular. (WBM.)

The cann[...]
because t[...]
were a few[...]
maintain[...]
pears was[...]
waterproo[...]
These wo[...]
jeans of a[...]
all require[...]

It was not uncommon to find giant trees in and around the valley. This specimen could probably produce enough lumber to build a house. Logging was a dangerous occupation requiring caution and skills. Many jobs could be found in the timber industry—from cutting to hauling to making lumber. (WBM.)

Birds Eye Snider Division of General Foods was next, and finally Agripac came on the scene. Birds Eye Cannery created many jobs while providing a place for farmers to sell their crops. There were men working to keep the place clean and repair machinery, while women worked on belts to remove stems, leaves, and other items that should not go into the cans. (DDP.)

North Marion Fruit

West Coast Fruit Growers Corporation, North Marion Fruit Company, and Smuckers also developed businesses locally. North Marion Fruit Company dealt mainly with berries and berry farmers. It also created part-time jobs to help the local economy. Berries were very fragile and needed to be handled quickly, usually during the night after they were picked during the day. In the beginning, berries were canned. Later, freezing berries became popular. (WBM.)

The cannery crew was mostly women because the jobs were seasonal. There were a few men who were managers and maintained the machinery. Canning pears was sometimes messy labor, so waterproof aprons kept the workers dry. These women still did not wear slacks or jeans of any kind while working. They were all required to wear hair nets. (WBM.)

It was not uncommon to find giant trees in and around the valley. This specimen could probably produce enough lumber to build a house. Logging was a dangerous occupation requiring caution and skills. Many jobs could be found in the timber industry—from cutting to hauling to making lumber. (WBM.)

One rarely sees giant logs like this anymore. There are very few stands of old-growth timber left to harvest. Today, most trees this size would be found in parks and state or federal forests. Many logging and mill jobs no longer exist, as much construction now uses various man-made materials. (WBM.)

Killian Smith (left) had a farm equipment business in Woodburn until he died quite suddenly, leaving his wife and seven children without a father and husband. The Smith family was the first and last family to live in the Settlemier House after Frank Settlemier died. Killian is on the left, consulting with a farmer about his tractor. (WBM.)

Steam engines like this were used in a variety of ways after they were developed. Steam energy replaced waterpower in factories. It began to replace horsepower on the farm. Later, machinery could move on its own power, and the first tractors began to appear. (WBM.)

Watermelons were a great crop here at one time. This man is proudly showing off his harvest of the tasty fruit. Stories abound of small neighborhood children raiding the neighbor's watermelon patch in the dark of night and getting caught by the farmer guarding his field. (OSL.)

Eight

RUSSIAN AND HISPANIC CULTURES

The Russian Old Believers in Woodburn are a minority group that first came to live here in about 1965. Their ancestors were Russian Orthodox Church members who refused to accept the Russian church reforms dictated by the church patriarch in the middle of the 17th century. They wanted to preserve the old ways, so they moved many times to find religious freedom in remote areas. They settled into isolated areas of the Russian Far East and Siberia, then into Poland, Romania, Turkey, and Central Asia.

The World Council of Churches helped to relocate the Russians to Brazil and Argentina. From there, many families discovered Russian-speaking Molokans in the Woodburn area and relocated to Oregon, where they purchased large tracts and started building houses and churches. While the Old Believers came from different parts of the world to meet in Oregon, their religious practices were almost identical. Many seem to have found the freedom they were looking for in the Willamette Valley; others moved on to more remote regions like Alaska.

The Treaty of Guadalupe Hidalgo, signed on February 2, 1848, gave the United States nearly half of the total area of Mexico. According to *Mexicans in Oregon*, by the Valley Migrant League, 80,000 people of Mexican descent became instant citizens of the United States. Spanish remains the first language for many in the Southwest even today.

Spanish-speaking migrant farmworkers first started arriving in Woodburn from Mexico under the Braceros Program during World War II. This arrangement helped the farmers harvest their crops when all their help was off to war. The Mexican workers returned to their homes in Mexico after harvest season. Braceros also worked in food processing plants.

After World War II, the program was phased out, and Woodburn was one of the places where migrant farm workers and their families came to work in seasonal crops. They lived in housing furnished by the farmers. Eventually, these migrant workers began to settle in more permanent housing and were hired to work all year on the farms. Their children were able to go to school for the full year, and many of them have now continued their educations in colleges and universities.

Each Old Believer home displays icons in a "beautiful corner." It is usually located in an eastern corner near the entrance to the home. Old Believer visitors first pray in front of the icon corner before greetings are made. Icons can also be mounted in the kitchen for prayers before and after meals and in bedrooms for prayers before bedtime and upon rising. (Courtesy of Richard Morris.)

The traditional priest-less marriage takes place at the prayer hall just after the all-night Sunday service during a time of non-fasting. From left to right, the best man; Sergei, the groom; Natali, the bride; a matron of honor from her family, and a matron of honor from his family are tied together with a string of kerchiefs for the entire first day of the wedding. This is an Old Believer custom. After marriage, women cover their hair. (RMP.)

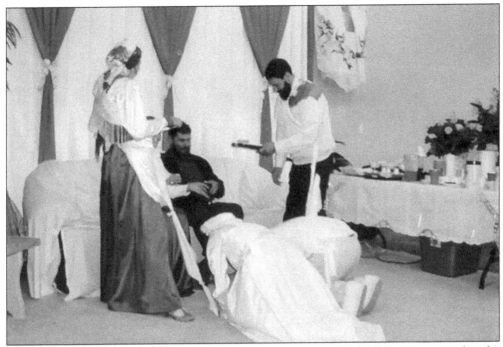

The bowing ceremony takes place before both sets of parents, with the best man seeing that the bride and groom pay their proper respects—especially if the gifts they receive from both parents are substantial. Many Russian Old Believers marry young, usually in their teens. (RMP.)

The men are resting after a long night of church services. Old Believer men never shave their facial hair after they marry, and women never cut their hair. A woman's hair is hidden under a kerchief and never seen by anyone outside the home. (RMP.)

The Alagoz family is one of the early Russian Old Believer families to move to Woodburn. Styles have changed very little in this c. 1970 photograph. The dresses worn by women have gotten a little longer than the ankle length shown in this picture. Otherwise, Old Believers dress the same as when they came to the Willamette Valley. (DDP.)

Men wear a tunic-type shirt with a woven belt around the waist. The women make all of the clothing for the entire family and carefully sew the shirts and embroider designs. They are excellent seamstresses, who use a unique needle and punch it up and down for solid embroidered decorations. Pictured are, from left to right, Makar and Caisia Zenukin and Tamara and Richard Morris. (RMP.)

Antonina (left) and Tamara Morris are picking berries for home use. Many Russians are excellent cooks and eat a healthy diet of fish, vegetables, and several Russian specialties. During many religious fast days, the women know exactly how to make the proper bread dough and meatless meals. (RMP.)

The women often get together and make dozens of *pil'meni* and other traditional foods which they can cook or freeze for later use. Pil'meni is pasta stuffed with meat or potatoes similar to ravioli. Once made, they are a fast food to cook and serve. (RMP.)

These women appear to be eager to get together and learn something new. Many find time between keeping house, taking care of children, cooking, and sewing to enjoy sharing knowledge with each other. They also work hard to acquire literacy in the language of the country where they are currently located. (RMP.)

Aleksandr Cain is giving a presentation in Russian. Old Believers want their children to be literate in Russian as well as in the language of their new country and the language of their church prayer books, Church Slavonic. Children work very hard to please their parents. (RMP.)

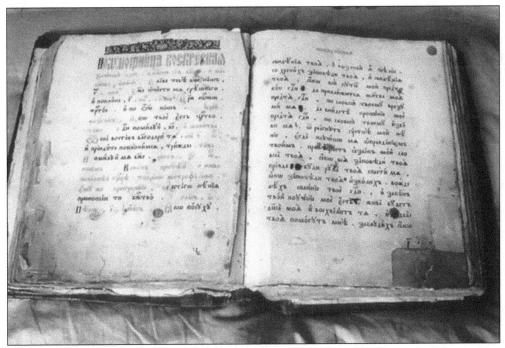

This is a well-worn prayer book with drops of candle wax from being read by candlelight at night. The corners are frayed and patched. This book is from the 17th century and is similar to those in use today. (RMP.)

There are two kinds of places of worship; those that have a priest who is under a bishop attend a church that has an altar. Those who appoint a leader to lead them with readings and prayers meet in a prayer hall. This church has a priest and is on Bethlehem Street on the outskirts of Woodburn. (WBM.)

This building is one of the prayer halls that have no officially ordained priest, but only a lay leader. Men stand on the right in church, and women are on the left side behind the men's choir while facing the front. There are no benches except for one along the sides and back for elderly members. (RMP.)

The inside of the church with a priest is ornate and covered with painted icons. Members of the congregation stand for hours and recites ancient prayers of their faith. Small children often move quietly between mother and father and rarely make a peep. (RMP.)

Many Hispanic workers would get jobs picking berries in the field. Their money would be pooled to buy the necessities. Crawling on the ground was not easy work, and the hours were long. Many times, the weather did not cooperate. (WBM.)

Migrant Hispanic farmworkers came to labor on large farms and were given housing for their families by the farm owners. Some chose to stay all year and eventually found local housing outside the camp to suit their family needs. This is a typical farm labor camp in the 1960s. (CLA.)

Many areas of Mexico have beautiful traditional costumes and original folk dances. This couple is enjoying a traditional dance. Folk dancers are a feature of the Woodburn Fiesta Mexicana each August. (Courtesy of Brenda Diaz.)

Many children start early to learn the traditional dances of their ancestral villages in Mexico. Emily Diaz is enjoying her costume and following in the steps of her big sisters. Thanks to the dedication of parents and others in the Hispanic community, it is delightful to watch girls like Emily perform. (Courtesy of Brenda Diaz.)

A Fiesta Mexicana has been held every year in Woodburn for over 50 years. It is colorful, the food is delicious, and the music is from south of the border. The event lasts for several days, with a big soccer tournament in the middle. People come from many towns to attend. Mr. and Mrs. ? Gonzales appears ready for the fun. (WBM.)

Children are ready to take off on a parade float that precedes the fiesta events. The parade is very colorful, with Hispanic families coming from long distances to attend the festivities. The fiesta grounds are filled with smells of tacos, burritos, and other Mexican delicacies. (Courtesy of Elida Sifuentez.)

La Posada is an event that happens in December before Christmas every year. Young people enact the plight of Mary and Joseph in looking for shelter and for baby Jesus. They go from house to house and usually find the baby on Christmas Eve in the church manger. (WBM.)

When a young Mexican girl reaches the age of 15, she can have a *quinceañera*. This is both a religious celebration and a coming out party that means she is now old enough to date. The girl wears a white formal dress and is attended by a number of friends and relatives all dressed formally. After the church service, there is a big reception and party. (Courtesy of Amalia Moreno.)

Traditionally, some Hispanics have been excellent cowboys and learned at an early age how to swing a lasso. There are some who work as real cowboys and others who just enjoy practicing the skills and entertaining. They often take part in rodeo parades. Here, Brenda Diaz is getting ready to ride in a parade. (Courtesy of Brenda Diaz.)

Here, boys and girls learn at an early age how to perform traditional Mexican folk dances from various regions of the country. It is fun to watch them and fun to join in at one of the festivals. In the United States, Cinco de Mayo (May 5) is a big celebration of Mexican culture, but it is not Mexican Independence Day. That occurs on September 16. (WBM.)

A Mexican wedding is usually a big affair. In addition to the traditional bridesmaids all wearing identical dresses, there is a group pictured here of the *padrinos*. In English, that would be "godparents." They furnish the necessities like the cake, the flowers, the candles, and so on for the ceremony. The groom's parents are responsible for the reception. (Courtesy of Elida Sifuentez.)

This mariachi band is composed of Mexican folk singers and musicians. They augment a Spanish-language church service and entertain at Mexican parties with their toe-tapping music. It is hard to sit still and just listen. The men use traditional guitars, violins, and occasionally folk instruments. And some fans claim the men's voices rival the Three Tenors. (Courtesy of Elida Sifuentez.)

Nine

SENIOR ESTATES GOLF AND COUNTRY CLUB

George Brice had an idea. He searched for land to build more than 1,000 small, affordable homes for retirees. After several setbacks, he chose to build in Woodburn. The first house was located on the corner of Highway 214 and Astor Way, and was finished in July 1960. Flooding from heavy rains delayed construction the first year. The housing area was slow to get started, but soon caught on like wildfire.

Much has happened since the first few houses were built in a swampy field. The city of Woodburn has more than tripled in size, and the land developed for people over 55 has become a comfortable neighborhood where seniors have their own country club, swimming pool, board of directors, newspaper, and 18-hole golf course. Thursday-morning coffee hours and local area potlucks keep residents in touch. The area has around 2,500 seniors living in the community and looking out for each other. This feeling is often missing in other cities and even in parts of Woodburn. Residents take time to know each other and check on their neighbors' needs.

The first families to move here, however, were impacted by the Columbus Day windstorm on Friday, October 12, 1962. People were without heat and cooking facilities until the electricity was restored. They were cold and hungry, but that did not slow the seniors down. Someone broke out a gas barbecue grill, and the entire neighborhood came for hot food and warm fellowship.

Retirement at Senior Estates offers the residents many choices, and there simply is not enough time in a day to participate in everything. They get out of the house to take part in exercises, walking clubs, dancing, parties, and trips. Many of them also volunteer in schools, the food bank, and other local churches and organizations. All these activities keep seniors going a little longer. Today, Senior Estates continues to add a slightly different dimension and culture to the growing city of Woodburn.

George Brice is selling a home to a prospective Senior Estates couple. The first residences in Senior Estates were rather small, less than 1,000 square feet, and there were four designs to choose from. In later years, larger houses were built and many residents remodeled their small homes in various creative ways. They all pay a yearly fee, and an elected board of directors administers the community covenants. (WBM.)

The clubhouse at Senior Estates offers many happy hours of fun and enjoyment. The building has been expanded as the community has grown. Activities are offered to those who are members of this unique village of people over 55 years of age. People outside the Estates can join in the activities by paying a yearly membership fee. (WBM.)

Here is what open house at Senior Estates looked like in the summer of 1960. People from throughout the United States received invitations to these events, and Senior Estates began to grow. As people moved in, they added onto their basic homes, and the community soon looked like a regular neighborhood instead of a housing development. (WBM.)

The private indoor swimming pool offers fun year-round. Here, seniors are playing a water volleyball game. There has always been a place in the gym or pool for active seniors to exercise. A walking club manages to find new and interesting places to walk. And many exercise classes take place in the clubhouse. (KLP.)

It is a real treat to golf in the sun in Oregon. The 18-hole golf course has encouraged people to buy houses in Senior Estates, and it helps keeps home values up for everyone. Not all people play golf, but there are many tournaments to involve those who enjoy the sport. (KLP.)

Golf carts come in handy for other things besides traveling the golf course. They are allowed to buzz around on streets inside Senior Estates. The carts can take seniors to the local shopping center and fast food outlets. Some are even used in walking dogs. (KLP.)

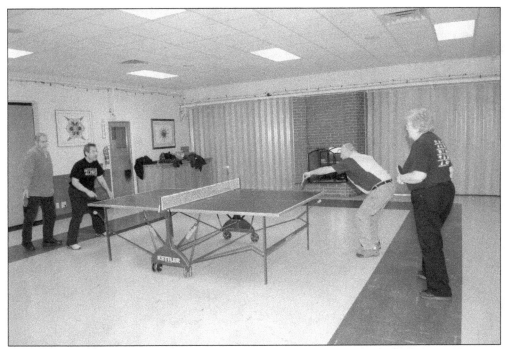

Ping-pong is a fast and active sport that can get one's heart rate up rapidly. A number of residents are passionate about playing, and there is much competition. One can be very active or just sit back and watch the action. (KLP.)

Some say that playing cards is good brain exercise. Several times a week, people get together to socialize and use their special skills to play pinochle and bridge. Meeting and visiting is half the fun of these get-togethers. (KLP.)

Those who live in Senior Estates, where a table is always waiting for those that are ready to play, need not venture to a pool hall. Besides games, there is a Thursday-morning coffee hour full of entertainment and ideas for trips. (KLP.)

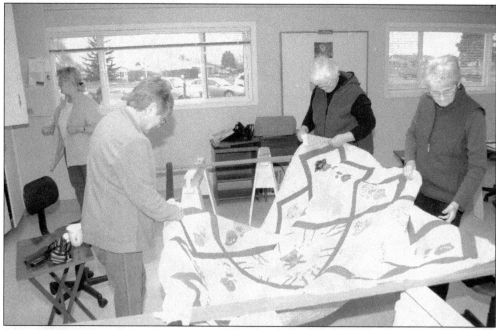

These ladies enjoy a little creativity while sewing quilts for those in need. Putting fabric together and choosing the right colors is a real art and certainly much appreciated by the people who benefit by the gifts that are turned out. These people not only help others, but they help themselves by getting out and doing something for others. (KLP.)

Exercising is a must to chase away the aches and pains, or sometimes to make new ones. There are a walking club and many types of exercises available, from easy to difficult. Getting up early is a discipline that is sometimes hard to manage for many. (KLP.)

Playing bingo is a real challenge with two or more cards. Win or lose, it is a good for seniors to get out of the house. One group has formed to actually make money for senior projects; it has been active for many years now. (KLP.)

Dancing is another of good exercise and also a way to meet others who enjoy the same activity. Many small musical groups play for the dances. There is a Golden Squares dance group that meets there also. The seniors keep busy with many activities. (KLP.)

An impromptu picnic brings out the neighbors. Many of the neighborhoods in Senior Estates hold monthly picnics or potlucks to meet and socialize. The events bring out the chefs with their delicious recipes, and one can try different foods without having to work in the kitchen all day. (WBM.)

Ten

A Few

Inspirational Residents

Woodburn did not just produce farm products and nursery stock. A whole library could be devoted to the many distinguished people who have called Woodburn home. These citizens include successful athletes, adventurers, military heroes, inventors, professionals, and worthy people who have worked to make their community, their state, and their country a better place. This chapter is an attempt to hit some high spots and remember some events of the past that have kept Woodburn in the news.

Listed under baseball greats from Woodburn are Bill Bevins, Clarence Charles Sauvain, Dick Whitman, and Tom Gorman. A "boxing family" included Tony Kahut, Eddie Kahut, and Joe Kahut Jr. Bill Austin played and coached football.

Marion Carl was a Marine helicopter pilot with many accomplishments in aviation history.

Marquis De Lafayette Remington started as a machine shop operator and experimented with steam engines that powered tractors.

There is a long list of those who used their talents to make Woodburn a better place, including Dr. Gerald Smith, a general practitioner who specialized in delivery babies and was known as "the baby doctor"; Nellie Muir, one of many outstanding teachers; Nancy Kirksey, a visionary who organized Woodburn Chemeketa Community College from her living room; the Reverend William Gordon MacLaren, a social worker who helped families and prisoners to get on the right path again; Walter Tooze, a politician and businessman; Elida Sifuentez, from an early migrant farm family, who became a nurse and a member of the Woodburn City Council; and Hazel Smith, who managed to save the Settlemier House for the community and to develop a unique subdivision, to name a few.

Stacey Allison became interested in climbing mountains and managed to reach the top of Mount Everest. She was the first American woman to accomplish this feat.

Floyd Clifford "Bill" Bevins (1916–1991) played American Legion baseball for Woodburn before becoming a professional. He is pictured here (third row, far right) in a 1935 Legion team photograph. In game four of the 1947 World Series, Bevins was one out away from pitching the first no-hitter in World Series history for the New York Yankees when Harry Arthur "Cookie" Lavagetto of the Brooklyn Dodgers stepped up to bat. Lavagetto sent the ball off into the right field wall and brought the tying run and the winning run into home. The Yankee catcher that day was a rookie named Yogi Berra. The Dodgers won that game, but the New York Yankees won the series. (Courtesy of Dennis Colgan.)

Marion Carl (1915–1998) learned to fly while in college. He graduated from Oregon State University in 1938 and joined the Army Reserve. In 1939, he enlisted in the Marine Corps. By the end of World War II, Carl had become an ace. He was the first Marine helicopter pilot to take off and land from an aircraft carrier, and he set a world speed record of 651 miles per hour on August 25, 1947. In August 1953, he set a world altitude record. In January 1964, Carl became commander of the 1st Marine Expedition Brigade in Vietnam and was pinned with his first gold star. He retired in 1973 with 13,000 flying hours and a chestful of medals. Major General Carl was fatally shot by an intruder while protecting his wife in his home in Roseberg, Oregon, on June 30, 1998, and was buried at Arlington National Cemetery in Virginia with full military honors at the age of 82. (Courtesy of the Marion Carl family.)

The prizefighting Kahut brothers were raised on a 103-acre farm just south of Woodburn. Three of the boys became interested in boxing at an early age. Joe Kahut Sr. is pictured here with three of his five boys and one girl. Tony Kahut (1918–1992), left, became the Oregon State and North West Middleweight Boxing Champion in 1940. After Pearl Harbor, Tony joined the Navy as a machinist mate and was serving on the USS *Nashville* when it carried Gen. Douglas MacArthur to Leyte. Tony returned home from military duty and operated a gas station on the corner of First and Lincoln Streets in downtown Woodburn for many years. Eddie Kahut (1930–), center, had his boxing career cut short in 1953 when he became involved in a traffic accident. That did not stop him from a love of boxing, and he used his talents to coach a boxing team at MacLaren Correctional School in Woodburn, where he worked as a counselor. Eddie recently organized a reunion for boxers that brought together many familiar names in the US boxing profession. Joe Kahut Jr. (1923–1990) is seen on the right. St. Luke Parish Hall became the hangout for at least 300 onlookers from priests, to cannery workers, mothers, a delegation from the Salem Chamber of Commerce, farmers, and children of all ages in the evenings to watch farm boy Joe Jr. practice his fighting techniques with trainers. The *Portland Oregonian* reported, "Joe Kahut will become Oregon's all-time No. 1 boxing attraction." And that prediction came true when "Joltin' Joe" was inducted into the Oregon Sports Hall of Fame in 1987. (Courtesy of Eddie Kahut.)

Don Burlingham was born in Portland, Oregon, June 2, 1926. A World War II veteran, he graduated from Oregon State College with a degree in business and technology in 1950. In 1941, his father had purchased Woodburn Fertilizer on Front Street (originally the Woodburn Flour Mill), and Don bought the business in 1963. He was named Junior First Citizen of Woodburn in 1961, and his talent for leadership grew as president of both the Jaycees and the Rotary Club, chairman of the Parks and Recreation Board, the United Good Neighbors local, and Marion/ Polk County UGN. He was elected to city council from 1962–1966 and was mayor for two terms from 1966–1970. In 1979, the Woodburn Chamber of Commerce voted him Retailer of the Year. The Rotary Club gave him the Vocational Senior Award in 1987 and the Agricultural Star Award in 1988. Don will always be remembered for his generosity and community interests. In 1970, he started donating trees to city parks and individual residents. In 1972, the Burlingham Agriculture Scholarships began providing students at Woodburn High School with $1,000 and $2,000 scholarships for majoring in agriculture at Oregon State University. Annually, Don gave $10,000 to the school district for computer education, and he frequently donated items from his business for various projects. He had a gift for helping people work together. His leadership, inspiration, and work ethic have made Woodburn a better place to live.

Clarence Charles "Chuck" Sauvain (1927–2006) excelled in basketball and baseball at Woodburn High School, where he graduated in 1945. After earning a degree in physical education from Oregon State University and playing college baseball, he signed with the Pittsburgh Pirates. Chuck was an outstanding southpaw pitcher. He was drafted into the Army, where he served with the military police during the Korean War era. Chuck gave up his promising baseball career to return home from military service and help his ailing father in the family business, Sauvain Ford Motor on the corner of Front and Harrison Streets in downtown Woodburn. (Courtesy of Tom Sauvain.)

Marquis De Lafayette Remington (1847–1897) crossed the plains in 1849 with his family. After living in various places on the West Coast, he moved in 1871 to Woodburn, where he became a blacksmith in the same year that Jesse Settlemier platted his first four blocks. In 1882, Remington started a machine shop located on Harrison Street between Front and First Streets called Woodburn Iron Works. He built his first steam engine in 1885 and was granted a patent for it in 1888. A fire destroyed the business in 1886, for a loss of $10,000 in building and machinery, so Remington relocated to Cleveland and Front Streets, where he continued to build his traction engines. He gained a reputation as a mechanical genius and designed a steam engine that could travel along while hauling loads. Two sets of gears were a feature that allowed for different speeds, and a differential was used to apply power to the drive wheels. Remington made five engines in Woodburn that proved themselves capable of hauling heavy loads up hills and down, but he soon realized he could not keep up with demand. He made a deal with the C.L. Best Tractor Company in San Leandro, California, to manufacture the engines. After several different mergers, the Best Company combined with Holt Manufacturing in 1925 to form the Caterpillar Tractor Co., now Caterpillar Inc., which still manufactures tractors and other industrial equipment. Remington and his son gave Harrison Street to the city of Woodburn in 1892. (WBM.)

Bill Austin (1928–), second from left, was a football giant at Woodburn High School and Oregon State College. He went on to play seven seasons, from 1949 to 1957, with the New York Giants. The team won the NFL Championship in 1956. He then became offensive line coach under Vince Lombardi (kneeling in front) of the Green Bay Packers from 1959 to 1964. Green Bay won the NFL championship in 1962. When Lombardi moved to the Washington Redskins, he brought Austin with him as assistant head coach. When Lombardi died, Austin became head coach of the Redskins. He was named to the Oregon Sports Hall of Fame in 1982. (WBM.)

Dick Whitman (1920–2003) went to the University of Oregon, graduated in 1942, and signed with the Brooklyn Dodgers. He joined the military in 1943–1945 and served in World War II at the Battle of the Bulge, where he received the Bronze Star and the Purple Heart. He played for the Dodgers from 1946 to 1949. In 1947–1949, he divided his time between Brooklyn and the Montreal Royals. In 1950–1951, he was with the Philadelphia Phillies; they won the 1950 National League Pennant. In 1952, Whitman came back to Portland and played with the Portland Beavers. He was a left fielder who batted left and threw the ball with his right hand. (WBM.)

Dr. Gerald Smith (1893–1984) was born and raised in Clinton, New Jersey. In 1925, he moved to Woodburn, where he is remembered as Woodburn's baby doctor. It is said that he delivered over 3,000 babies. He made many house calls and also preformed over 3,000 surgeries. His office was in the Association Building when he was not delivering babies or working in the hospital. He took over the 10-bed Woodburn Hospital in the late 1930s and began recruiting other doctors to help him. Smith never missed a Woodburn High School sports game and became the team doctor. He was the doctor for MacLaren School for Boys from 1941 to 1966. He served as Woodburn's health officer and was a charter member of the Woodburn Rotary Club. He retired in 1971 at the age of 78 due to ill health, and concentrated on his stamp collection. In 1984, the Woodburn High School football stadium received a new name, Dr. Gerald Smith Stadium, in his honor. (WBM.)

The hospital on First and Hayes Streets had 10 beds and was mostly a maternity center. The Salem Hospitals were better prepared for serious illnesses, and Dr. Gerald Smith would often use his station wagon as an ambulance to take patients for more extensive treatments. Here, the American Legion Auxiliary is marching past the hospital during a parade. (WBM.)

Rev. William Gordon MacLaren was born in Scotland and came to Chicago in 1893 to sell tea and coffee for an import company. He attended Moody Bible Institute and was later ordained as a Free Methodist minister. He arrived in Portland in 1905 and worked in groceries and merchandising until 1907, when he sold his business and devoted his life to missions and rescue work. MacLaren was committed to helping those with mental and moral needs. His work with those in prison and those discharged as well as with the families of prisoners was so outstanding that it was determined that the MacLaren Youth Correctional Facility in Woodburn would be renamed after him. (Courtesy of the Old Kerr Nursery Association and Albertina Kerr Centers for Children.)

In 1957, shortly before she died, Nellie Muir (1874–1962) was presented with the Woodburn Chamber of Commerce Distinguished Service Award, becoming the first woman to be so honored. She moved to Woodburn in 1924 with her husband, a retired rancher who became the street commissioner in Woodburn before he died in 1943. Nellie worked in Woodburn grade schools for 25 years before retiring in 1949. What made her outstanding was her unlimited generosity. Many of Nellie's gifts of time and money were anonymous. She made sure her students had enough food and clothing and medical attention, with the help of Dr. Gerald Smith. She also taught in two different churches' Sunday schools. Nellie died in 1962, not knowing that a school would be named for her. (DDP.)

When Killian Smith, then manager of the International Harvester dealership in Woodburn, decided his family needed to move to Woodburn to be closer to his business, his wife, Hazel (1919–), told him she would only move if he could find a farm. He located the 240-acre Jesse Settlemier farm with its Queen Anne–style mansion on Settlemier Avenue for sale, and Hazel said yes. They moved in 1952. Killian died quite suddenly of a heart attack in 1963. Hazel had seven children to raise. She sold the implement dealership because International Harvester was reluctant to let a woman manage one of its franchises, and she began subdividing the farm. The area known as Smith Addition is today considered one of the nicest housing areas and neighborhoods in Woodburn. In this February 1973 picture, taken just before the family moved out of the Settlemier House, are, from left to right, (first row) Glen, Hazel, and Martha; (second row) Rita, Lana, Ruth, Nina, and Yvonne. The house then sold to the newly formed French Prairie Historical Society. (Courtesy of the Smith family and Stefani and Daniel Photography.)

In 1988, Stacy Allison became the first American woman to conquer Mount Everest. Her first attempt in 1987 had failed. Two Canadian climbers accompanied her to the summit on this second trip. Unfortunately, one of the Canadians lost his life on the way back down. About 2,000 feet below the top, Allison had to stop while 75-mile-per-hour winds began roaring past. Before climbing Everest, she conquered Mount McKinley and K2. A city street in Woodburn bears her name. When she is not climbing, Allison manages a construction business in Portland and does many motivational speaking engagements throughout the year. (WBM.)

It must be the Woodburn water that produces such outstanding baseball players. Tom Gorman, a left-handed pitcher and batter, grew up in Woodburn, went to Gonzaga University in Spokane, Washington, and played for the Montreal Expos in 1980–1982. He was traded to the New York Mets in 1982–1985. In 1986, he was released from his contract and signed as a free agent with the Philadelphia Phillies. In 1987, he signed with the San Diego Padres and was traded to the Minnesota Twins. Gorman played a few months with that team before retiring from baseball. (Courtesy of the Gorman family.)

The Produce Merchandise King of French Prairie is an example of the self-made men who helped to develop the early city of Woodburn. He did many different jobs to make a living and was good at all of them. Walter Tooze was left an orphan at five and lived with an uncle. The family arrived in Portland from Ohio in 1877 when he was 17. He worked on a dairy farm, and then moved to Newberg and cleared 50 acres of brush with an axe while teaching at a school on Parrott Mountain. In 1884, he went into the mercantile business in Butteville with J. Barnes, who later became his father-in-law. In 1890, Tooze became the postmaster in Woodburn and built a structure on Front Street. He opened the Palace Bazaar store, where he did a record business. A staunch Republican, he served a term as mayor of Woodburn. Tooze had a habit of wearing his overcoat like a cape, with the sleeves flowing behind him. He loved to speak and was asked to give an address at centennial of the Lewis and Clark Exposition in Portland on "Woodburn Day" in 1905. The cigar he is smoking in the picture is probably one of Ed Becker's creations. (WBM.)

Nancy Kirksey, right, started the Woodburn Chemeketa Community College satellite center from her living room in 1977. The college center was moved to a modular classroom behind the high school and eventually to a small building on Lincoln Street next to the railroad tracks. Nancy served eight years as mayor of Woodburn, the first woman to hold this office. She was born and raised in Maine before coming to Oregon. Nancy has two married sons and four grandchildren. She and her husband, Loy, have been married 49 years. Elida (Bustamante) Sifuentez, left, came from Asherton, Texas, with her migrant family who found work and lived on a farm in St. Paul, Oregon, while she was growing up. She became a nurse and worked at Newberg Hospital for a while and then was hired as a nurse at MacLaren Correctional Facility in Woodburn for 35 years before retiring. She was the Hispanic voice on the Woodburn City Council for 23 years. She and her husband, Jose Sifuentez, have three grown children and four grandchildren and have been married 38 years. (Courtesy of Elida Sifuentez.)

Visit us at
arcadiapublishing.com

Printed in the USA
CPSIA information can be obtained
at www.ICGtesting.com
LVHW070742121223
766160LV00008B/94